HOW TO ANALYZE PEOPLE

*How to Master Reading Anyone Instantly
Using Body Language, Human Psychology,
and Personality Types*

© **Copyright 2017 by Ryan James - All rights reserved.**

The following Book is reproduced below with the goal of providing information that is as accurate and as reliable as possible. Regardless, purchasing this Book can be seen as consent to the fact that both the publisher and the author of this book are in no way experts on the topics discussed within, and that any recommendations or suggestions made herein are for entertainment purposes only. Professionals should be consulted as needed before undertaking any of the action endorsed herein.

This declaration is deemed fair and valid by both the American Bar Association and the Committee of Publishers Association and is legally binding throughout the United States.

Furthermore, the transmission, duplication or reproduction of any of the following work, including precise information, will be considered an illegal act, irrespective whether it is done electronically or in print. The legality extends to creating a secondary or tertiary copy of the work or a recorded copy and is only allowed with express written consent of the Publisher. All additional rights are reserved.

The information in the following pages is broadly considered to be a truthful and accurate account of facts, and as such any inattention, use or misuse of the information in question by the reader will render any resulting actions solely under their purview. There are no scenarios in which the publisher or the original author of this work can be in any fashion deemed liable for any hardship or damages that may befall them after undertaking information described herein.

Additionally, the information found on the following pages is intended for informational purposes only and should thus be considered, universal. As befitting its nature, the information presented is without assurance regarding its continued validity or interim quality. Trademarks that mentioned are done without written consent and can in no way be considered an endorsement from the trademark holder.

Table of Contents

INTRODUCTION: The Importance of Analyzing Others Instantly 1

CHAPTER 1: Identifying Personality Types 18

CHAPTER 2: The Principles of Perceptions 41

CHAPTER 3: Body Language Speaks Volumes 53

CHAPTER 4: Interpreting and Responding to the Message 69

CHAPTER 5: Three Key Elements to Connectivity 82

CHAPTER 6: The Beauty of Successfully Analyzing Others 91

Congratulations on Your Read 95

INTRODUCTION

THE IMPORTANCE OF ANALYZING OTHERS INSTANTLY

When communicating with others, we have become extraordinarily dependent upon just what we see and hear on the surface. However, just below the shallows is a whole other world of motivations that direct behaviors and determine the effectiveness of our perceptions. Often others' surface expressions, words, and actions are not congruent to what is happening on that deeper level. To be dynamic communicators, we need to have "deep see" vision to analyze others real motives and reason behind what they say and do. Not only will analyzing others give us a more accurate perception of them, but it will also give us greater insight into ourselves.

Have you ever felt an almost uncanny creepiness about a person or an immediate kinship with someone, but you have no clear explanation as to why? That's because you were sensitive to other non-verbal signals, behaviors, and traits that the other person was so desperately wanting to hide to gain your trust. Once you train yourself to be mindful of others' covert messages, you'll have much more confidence in your perceptions and ability to handle almost any situation before it becomes threatening to your well-being. So, let's look at what learning to analyze others can do for us.

Accurately Analyzing Others Can Keep Us Physically Safe

Linda is an excellent example of how carefully analyzing others can protect you. As a Realtor® for over ten years, Linda attributed much of her success on her strong communication skills. She had been told on numerous occasions that she was a good judge of character, and it had paid off in spades. When she was with clients, it was as if she knew what her prospects were going to say or do before they knew. One afternoon, these skills served a far greater purpose than merely winning her the contract.

Each morning she had coffee on her way to work. It was a great way to socialize and pass out her business cards. As Linda waited in line for her coffee, she struck up a conversation with the gentleman behind her. As usual, she gave him her business card, and he immediately shared his need to sell his home and move into something larger. He had just been promoted at work and wanted his lifestyle to reflect his new position, and Linda was eager to help him search for the perfect home. He gave her his address, and they arranged to meet the next day at his home with a current market analysis to determine its value.

Never suspecting danger, Linda went by herself to his home, knocked at the front door with her usual confidence, and waited for his invitation to enter. He welcomed her into the home and stepped behind her to lock the front door. She immediately felt this was a bit odd but dispelled the feeling in hopes that it was out of habit rather than a need to trap her inside his home. As she looked around, she noticed no sign of a feminine touch, with the minimal furnishings showing nothing but masculine appeal.

Unable to rid herself of the creep factor, Linda began to ask questions. "I'm ashamed of myself, but I didn't even get your name yesterday." She held out her hand to introduce herself—"Hi, I'm Linda, and, you are?"

"Oh—Jeff. My name's, Umm, Jeff," he replied, as he looked down at his feet. As if remembering he should behave differently, Jeff then looked up and smiled and offered his hand. That's when Linda noticed something else that was odd. His hand was clammy as if his nerves were getting the better of him. Upon closer inspection, she also noticed that although Jeff offered a smile in response, it was tight and didn't reach all the way to his eyes.

"Hello, Jeff," she smiled back, trying not to show her nervousness. "Do you mind if I look around so I can get an idea of the value of your house?"

"Oh, right—right," he said, walking behind her in a herding manner, and moving closely behind her toward the hallway.

"Well, let's start out here in the living area and kitchen, shall we?" As she passed the hall, her neck hairs began to stand to attention, and she went on full alert. The first room to the right of the hallway was entirely black, and she caught a glimpse of the corner of a daybed with a pink boa draped across its sidearm. It was difficult for Linda to hide her dismay at the sight of this little island of femininity in Jeff's otherwise overly masculine house.

Linda continued to take notes as she walked around the kitchen, asking light questions to try to keep the conversation casual. The quieter the two of them became, the louder Linda's little voice in her head shouted for her to get out of there. "You know, it got chilly this morning. I have such allergies in changing weather like this. Would you have some tissue?"

"Oh, yeah, he moved once again to position himself at her back awkwardly. Come on back," he said, as he then moved around her to walk down the hallway.

"Why don't you get some, and I'll get my jacket in the car?" The moment Jeff began walking down the hall, Linda made her getaway. Thankfully, she maneuvered herself between Jeff and the locked front door but opened the deadbolt quickly. She quickly grabbed her briefcase and car keys from the side table, ran to her car, and pulled out of Jeff's driveway as if the devil himself were after her.

Upset and shaken, Linda immediately reported her fear and behavior to her broker, warning other females not to go to that address alone. She wanted to call the police, but there was nothing to report, so she shook off her feeling of foreboding and took off the rest of the afternoon. Three nights later, Linda realized how close she had come to the horrific realization of her feelings that all was not as it should be at Jeff's house. As she watched the 10:00 news, she saw police leading Jeff out of his house in handcuffs, and the anchor people sadly reported his connection to two murdered women on the west side of the city.

Linda called the police and shared her story, and as she told them what happened, she realized that her analysis of Jeff had been spot on, but it was not what he said that had tipped her off to his possible deviant plans. It was how he behaved, what she observed, and her overall perceptions that signaled the alarm. Linda knew that she had always been able to read others well, but this time her intuitive perceptions had done more than fund her life—they had saved her life!

Analyzing Others Can Bring Us Professional Prosperity

James had never considered himself a natural born leader, but he had been asked to act as company vice president after the unexpected departure of his boss. He dreaded the first office meeting when he would have to share with the team that he was now the new vice president. James just knew that everybody had loved Eddie. He had a quick wit and a welcoming smile, always inviting others to participate and share their feelings about any new ideas or required changes. He gave the salespeople full reign to do their thing, and the team seemed to enjoy the freedom.

James, on the other hand, was a quiet contemplator. He knew that his discomfort with public speaking and quick decision making had negatively impacted several potential promotions for him throughout the years. Now that James finally had the opportunity to lead, he couldn't help but feel out of his comfort zone. James was shocked that he had been chosen for the position, and second to his disbelief was his feelings of inadequacy and unpreparedness. Just two months previously, James had attended a communications seminar where the speaker talked about the effects of misunderstandings in the workplace. Now James wondered if others would mistake his quiet demeanor and reticent manner as a lack of leadership skills.

James welcomed the opportunity to promote his assistant to become the new executive assistant to the vice president, knowing her strengths were his weaknesses. She was confident, outgoing, and easily trusted when James tended to hang back. Yes, Susan would be the perfect complement to him in this new position, and he looked forward to having her input. As it turned out, James fears were put to rest when the team began to flourish under his gentle guidance and Susan's nurturing nature.

Together, they created stability in the sales team and encouraged even greater participation and higher-level contributions from all parties. It seemed the wrong perceptions were on James part. What he believed everybody thought was real leadership had been a gathering of the "good ole boys" club, where little was expected and even less achieved. In record time, the salespeople thrived under James leadership and his assistant's support. James' confidence and performance were surprisingly successful in creating peak performance for the entire team, and he and Susan worked together to build the highest selling team in the company.

There are many other ways analyzing people can benefit you. Learn and apply the strategies in our book, and you'll gain a new perspective on yourself and others. When you begin reading others and yourself with an open mind and willing spirit, your new skills will lead you to even greater successes in your personal and professional lives. Your relationships will improve, your confidence will increase, and your analytical knowledge will open doors for you that you never dreamed possible.

Analyzing Others Can Give Insight in Your Personal Relationships

For the longest time, the HOA board meetings had consisted of Ally and her husband. Until Theresa came along, nobody had been interested in the need to keep the greenbelts clean and the streetlights were working. Ally was a contradiction of feelings; although it was great to have another's opinion, she felt somewhat uncomfortable around Theresa. After the board meeting one evening, Theresa was on her way home when Ally's husband offered her a ride.

Nothing seemed out of the ordinary on the surface, but Ally felt wary of Theresa around her husband, Eddie. When she voiced her feelings to Eddie, he brushed her off and said something sarcastic about seeing her claws come out whenever Theresa was in the room. The more Ally tried not to let things bother her, the more the thoughts rolled around in her head. Perhaps it was because Eddie had worked so much overtime the last two weeks, and his boss was so selfish in his overtime pay that created such suspicious thoughts in Ally.

The next morning, Ally was checking the sprinklers out front when her neighbor walked over and told her something that confirmed her fears. The friend told Ally she had asked Eddie to say hello the other night when he was standing outside Theresa's house. "Oh, what night was that?" Ally asked.

"I went by the night before last, and he was standing outside Theresa's with a big box in his hands. I wondered if she was moving."

"I don't know." Ally was so upset that she excused herself and went into the house quickly before her neighbor could see her tears. The rest of the day was spent wondering what she was going to do. She wasn't going to put up with a cheating husband, but she just couldn't imagine herself without Eddie. It was her birthday, no less, and Eddie hadn't even wished her a happy birthday before going to work that morning. She just could face the heartache of telling him she knew, so she left before he could get home. As Ally passed Theresa's street, she noticed Eddie's car parked in front. Too hurt to stop and too mad not to, Ally decided she would put an end to this behavior and stop Eddie in his tracks.

She quickly ran to the front door, not realizing what a mess she looked with her makeup smeared and her hair still wet at the temples for trying to clean her face up before leaving the house. Nobody answered, so she rang the doorbell once again, and this time Eddie came to the door. "What are you doing here, honey?" Eddie took one look at her and knew she must be having an emergency. "What's wrong? Are you hurt?"

"You might say that, Eddie." Ally waved her arms in the air and continued with "I'm hurt about all this. How could you do this?" she asked, before bursting into tears.

Eddie grabbed her by the arm and pulled her into Theresa's house. "Okay, okay, what's all this about? What do you think I'm doing?"

"I've seen how you two look at each other as if you've got a secret you don't want anybody else to know about."

Theresa came out from the other room and walked over to Ally, "We do. We've been planning your surprise birthday party for the past two weeks."

Ally's misunderstanding had caused her pain and hurt, and it could have been the end of her marriage. Relationships are made and broken by poor communications and false perceptions. We would probably be shocked at how many couples had split because of mistaken beliefs caused by unfounded suspicions, as well as how many others were able to mislead their significant other and hold a shaky relationship together through deceit and negative manipulation.

These are the reasons we've written this book on how to analyze others. You'll learn to be more decisive, and rely on your perceptions to give you clarity in your personal and professional life. It won't take long before the benefits of that "deeper see" vision pays off in longer-lasting, more rewarding relationships and more profitable business associations. So, let's get started, shall we?

FREE BONUS BOOK

As a Thank You for purchasing this book, I would like to offer you another book as a special bonus. It is called *"The Secrets Behind Subtle Psychology: Secrets To Getting All You Want"*.

This comprehensive book is for those who are interested in:

- Learning more about Human Psychology and how it works

- Becoming more effective in your conversations

- Improving your social skills

- Learning about NLP (Neuro-Linguistic Programming) and how to use it to your benefit

- Improving on your Persuasion skills

- Improving your sales skills and closing more deals

- Becoming more influential

- And much more..

So if you are interested in learning more about any of the above, just go to http://bit.ly/subtlepsychology and grab your free bonus book!

CHAPTER 1

IDENTIFYING PERSONALITY TYPES

Even though there are four main personality types, most people are a combination of two or more types. You might be primarily one type with a few traits of another, or you could be middle of the road between two different types. There are also some people who have a few traits of every type. Several things determine your personality types, but the strongest influences are typically one's upbringing, hormones, and chemical makeup.

If you read my other book *How to Analyze People: How to Read Anyone Instantly Using Body Language, Personality Types and Human Psychology,* then you might already be familiar with these four personality types. In this chapter, we'll review the different personality types and go into greater detail about the positive and negative traits of each types, and their identifying behaviors and language.

Knowing others personality types and identifying behaviors and language that are characteristic of these types of people will help you know how best to relate to them in your personal and professional endeavors. After you have studied the personality types, take the time to do a personal inventory to discover your personality type. Knowing how you prefer to relate to others and how they want you to relate to them is paramount in making the necessary adjustments to the way you communicate with people of all different personality types and traits.

The Leader Personality Type

Leader Personality Types make great presidents and executives, administrators and wall street moguls, or managers and supervisors. Many politicians are Leader Personalities as well.

Positive Traits of a Leader Personality Type

Confident >> Direct >> Strategic >> Problem-Solver

Decisive >> Driven >> Courageous >> Bold

Independent >> Goal-Oriented >> Money-Oriented >> Proud

Energetic >> Focused >> Competitive >> Hard-Working

Powerful >> Tough >> Determined >> Take Charge

Negative Traits of a Leader Personality Type

Tense >> Workaholic >> Opinionated >> Temperamental

Stressed >> Too Controlling >> Power Hungry >> Too Authoritative

Rude >> Aggressive >> Judging >> Unforgiving

Distrusting >> Unavailable >> Detached >> Unsocial

Impatient >> Self-Centered >> Overly Competitive >> Stubborn

Identifying Behaviors of a Leader Personality Type

- They don't take a lot of time for family and friends.

- Most of their conversations center around work and money-making ventures.

- They respect strength and competitiveness, so they will usually be sports-minded and fit.

- They have a strong, confident handshake.

- Since they are money-motivated, they will usually drive an expensive car, live in a luxurious estate, and wear designer watches.

- They don't have much patience with people who don't display appreciation for the finer things in life.

- They are attracted to intelligent people and usually will not associate with others whom they feel are not on their level.

- Their body language is often a wide stance with arms folded in front of them or braced at the waist.

- It will be difficult for them to focus on conversations that don't center around work or intellectual matters.

Identifying Language of a Leader Personality Type

I   My   Intellect   Ambition   Challenge

The Identifier Personality Type

Identifier Personality Types are especially caring and nurturing people. They love nothing more than to educate, help, or heal others. These personality types make outstanding teachers, nurses, and counselors.

Positive Traits of an Identifier Personality Type

Nurturing >> Encouraging >> Sympathetic >> Cooperative

Understanding >> Relational >> Expressive >> Unassuming

Considerate >> Charitable >> Soul Searching >> Trusting

Good Listeners >> Compassionate >> Agreeable >> Empathetic

Emotional >> Imaginative >> Idealistic >> Contributors

Negative Traits of an Identifier Personality Type

Over-Thinkers >> Drama Queens >> Sacrificial >> Imbalanced Lifestyle

Appear Needy >> Too Agreeable >> Indecisive >> Demand Reassurance

Unfocused >> Too Accepting >> Take on Problems of the Universe

Identifying Behaviors of an Identifier Personality Type

- Because Identifier Personality Types don't want to offend others, they are often too agreeable.

- They are most susceptible to suffering depression or moodiness.

- They do not take criticism well; they become too easily offended.

- If they are in a managing position, they prefer an open-door policy.

- Their managing style is more open and relaxed.

- If they fear confrontation or rejection in social situations, they can appear shy and timid.

- Their body language is usually open arms and trusting mannerisms.

- They can be a bit touch-feely for other's taste.

- They are comfortable talking about emotions and their warm and fuzzy conversations often center around feelings and charitable events.

Identifying Language of an Identifier Personality Type

Passion > Sensitive > Sweet > Understand > Sorry

The Fraternizer Personality Type

Fraternizer Personality Types enjoy high adventure and challenging themselves with almost everything. They are real sensation seekers whose hunger for the unconventional adventure is their ultimate enjoyment. You will usually find Fraternizer Personality Types working as comedians, entertainers, event planners, venue coordinators, or even travel guides.

Positive Traits of a Fraternizer Personality Type

Friendly >> Storytellers >> Energetic >> Charming

Spontaneous >> Curious >> Engaging >> Outspoken

Social Butterfly >> Outgoing >> Optimistic >> Adaptable

Conversationalist >> Athletic >> Humorous >> Fun-loving

Enthusiastic >> Knowledgeable >> Creative >> Unconventional

Negative Traits of a Fraternizer Personality Type

Too Talkative >> Doesn't Listen >> Self-Centered >> Unfocused

Easily Bored >> Impulsive >> Restless >> Self-Absorbed

Procrastinator >> Low Tolerance >> Scattered >> Uncalculated Risk Taker

Identifying Behaviors of a Fraternizer Personality Type

- They love to travel and talk about their adventures.

- Fraternizers enjoy outdoor adventures, and they're always up for something out-of-the-norm.

- They are not afraid to speak their minds, even if they hold the unpopular opinion. Usually, they get others to agree with them just because they are so likable.

- They are big spenders. Fraternizers will usually pick up the tab for dinner or drinks.

- Because they are so impulsive and social, they are often more susceptible to drug and alcohol abuse.

- It can be challenging getting them to settle down to find a solution to a pressing problem.

- Most Fraternizers have bigger-than-life gestures and expressions.

Identifying Language of a Fraternizer Personality Type

Adventure >> Energy >> New >> Fun >> Wealthy

Pleasure >> Happiness >> Travel >> Active >> Why Not?

The Perceiver Personality Type

Perceiver Personality Types are your more serious-minded of the four main personality types. Because they are so fact-driven, they are quite often engineers, mathematicians, scientists, and technology experts.

Positive Traits of a Perceiver Personality Type

Organized >> Purpose-Driven >> Concentrated >> Logical

Analytical >> Task-Oriented >> Factual >> Orderly

Predictable >> Detail-Oriented >> Structured >> Dependable

Deep Thinker >> Investigative >> Patient >> Persistent

Sentimental >> Respectful >> Reliable >> Planner

Negative Traits of a Perceiver Personality Type

Unemotional >> Too One-minded >> Loner >> Too Serious

Unsocial >> Cold >> Predictable >> Anxious

Dogmatic >> Hard to Please >> Obsessive >> Stubborn

Identifying Behaviors of a Perceiver Personality Type

- Since they value being thoughtful and self-controlled, they express themselves using very precise language.

- They don't work well with demanding deadlines, and they are challenged with high-pressure tasks.

- They can be obsessive/compulsive in their behaviors.

- They can often be judging and critical of others.

- They are uncomfortable being the center of attention, so you will usually find them standing in the back of the group or crowd.

- They don't know how to take compliments and show embarrassment when given one.

- Since they are such deep thinkers, they don't usually make quick decisions or act quickly in an urgent situation.

- Perceivers will be the ones who hold you up in the grocery line to count out the exact change.

- Their body language is closed, and you will often notice that they avoid making eye contact.

Identifying Language of a Perceiver Personality Type

Respect >> Moral >> Loyalty >> Careful >> Count on Me

Taking a Personal Inventory of Your Personality Type

Answer the following questions to discover your personality type or types. Circle the letter that best describes your feelings, thoughts, or behaviors in the given situations. When you have completed the personal inventory, tally up your points to see your most likely personality type(s).

1. When you're in a meeting, you usually…

   a. Try to get everybody to participate

   b. Be quiet and let others do the talking

   c. Act like I agree even if I don't so I won't be confrontational

d. Offer my feelings on the subject and encourage others to as well

2. If your significant other is angry or frustrated, you …

   a. Suggest an evening out on the town to relieve the stress

   b. Go to my office for a while until he or she cools down

   c. Feel bad and wonder what I did wrong

   d. Let them think it out and then ask some pointed questions to seek closure

3. If your computer is acting up, you most likely would…

   a. Search the manual or the Internet for the problem, carefully weigh the suggested remedies, and then try the most likely solution

   b. Call a friend to come over for a drink and see what they can do to help me fix it

   c. I get the IT guy at work to come over and fix it

   d. I chat online and see if others are having the same issues and then try some of the things that helped them overcome the problem

4. If you get stood up for an evening out, what do you do?

   a. Call another friend and go somewhere with them instead.

   b. I enjoy the evening by myself at home.

   c. I ask them if there is anything I can do to help them with whatever it was that kept them from enjoying an evening with me.

   d. I do some work at home and get a head start on the next day's tasks.

5. When you lose a bet or a competition of some kind, you might…

   a. Double down—I hate to lose

   b. Wonder if they somehow cheated

   c. Be happy for my competitor

   d. Laugh it off and get ready for the next bet

6. If someone tries to tell you what to do, you usually …

   a. Listen to what they say, and then figure it out for myself anyway

   b. Understand they have experienced this before and try to do what they suggest

   c. I think they've got their nerve and do what I want

   d. Make a joke about it and then wait until they leave and ask someone else to do it for me

7. If you told your significant other you didn't want a dog and he or she got one anyway, you would most likely…

   a. Smile and start playing with the dog.

   b. Try to be sensitive to their need for a dog and think of how I can help take care of it

   c. Remember what happened the last time he or she got a dog and then remind them of what a disaster it was

   d. Make them take the dog back from whence it came

8. If you paid to have your car detailed and they didn't do a good job, you would most likely…

   a. Realize that they usually did a good job and just live with it

   b. Be upset with them and make them do the whole thing over

c. Kid around with them and ask them to touch it up in spots

d. I would give myself time to think about what I wanted to say and then take it back the next day and ask them to make it right

9. If you were dressed for and on your way to work and saw that your car had a flat tire in the driveway, you would…

a. Call a company to fix the tire and work from home until it was repaired

b. Call a friend or my significant other and ask what I should do

c. Call into work and let them know, call a repair company, and then go for a run until it was fixed

d. Look at the tire to see if it was tampered with, and then have it fixed, but I would be watching the street to see if anyone else was having a similar problem

10. If your child got a poor grade on his or her report card, AGAIN, you would most likely…

   a. Sit down with them and listen to their explanation and then figure out with them how they could do better next time

   b. Depend on my significant other to handle the situation

   c. Offer them some money to do better

   d. Probably blow up and let them know who's boss

Scoring—Discover Your Personality Type(s)

Give yourself a point under each appropriate personality type and then tally your points to see what personality type is dominant and which ones are secondary.

Question	Leader	Identifier	Fraternizer	Perceiver
#1	A	B	D	C
#2	B	C	A	D
#3	C	D	B	A
#4	D	C	A	B
#5	A	C	D	B
#6	C	B	D	A
#7	B	B	A	C
#8	D	A	C	D
#9	A	B	C	B
#10	D	A	C	B

Under which personality type(s) did you have the most circles? The personality type with the most circles is probably your dominant personality type, and those with just a few circles have some influence in your behaviors and beliefs.

Now comes the big surprise. Even though you took this Personal Inventory and you "think" you are predominantly one personality type, you might find out differently when it comes to what you'll discover in the next chapter. It's all about perception. How you perceived yourself might be much different than how others see you. So, let's explore the principles of perception and see what influence these perceptions have on the way we analyze ourselves and others.

CHAPTER 2

THE PRINCIPLES OF PERCEPTIONS

As you analyze others and yourself, you begin to form temporary and long-lasting perceptions. These truths are invaluable to get an accurate read of others and examine what motivates others' behaviors and beliefs. However, there are some universal truths about perceptions, and we call these the Principles of Perceptions. As you read others' body language and analyze their behaviors, keep the following Five Principles of Perceptions in mind. Knowing them will help your analysis to be more accurate.

Principle #1: Perceptions Are Deceptive

There is much information that goes into your analysis of yourself and others. However, it's not good practice to blindly accept the information that filters through your mind to create your perceptions. Why? To form your opinions of others while you analyze their behaviors and beliefs, you are working with a limited amount of knowledge and awareness. The following strategies will offer a more accurate analysis and verify or replace your initial perceptions.

- Spending more time with the people you are analyzing to form your impressions gives you a more precise read on their behaviors and beliefs. When you jump to conclusions about what motivates people to say or do things, you are playing off old tapes of past experiences. Your judgments can be tainted because of previous experiences you had when another person said or did similar things.

- Observing how others react to the people you are reading helps you to know whether you are too critical or judging of them. You need to ask yourself if your opinions of this person are based on personal likes or dislikes, or are your perceptions based on unbiased observations and effective listening skills.

- Have you rushed to judgment? When you are analyzing others, give them time to prove or disprove your perceptions of them. Avoid forming your analysis on just one or two encounters. If you must analyze another's behavior quickly, realize that there's a good chance your perceptions will not be entirely accurate.

Principle #2: Background Brings Accuracy

There are times when you must analyze others' behaviors quickly, but when you do your perceptions might be off the mark. After all, you have no background on this person and no history with which to form your impressions. For example, if you are in a group and someone moves away from you to stand on the other side of the group, what do you think? If you rush to judgment, you might believe that they are giving you the cold shoulder. Or, if you have experienced recent rejection, you might begin to wonder what is wrong with you. What you don't know when analyzing others can and will hurt your ability to form accurate perceptions.

Let's say this situation goes a little further and the person you are examining turns her head away from you. It's easy to convince yourself she is avoiding you—until you find out later in the evening that your subject suffered a severe hearing loss and needed to move closer to the speaker and tilt her head to hear better from her functioning ear. Suddenly, your perceptions of that person have drastically changed. Why? You have more background information.

Principle #3: Awareness & Accuracy Go Hand-in-Hand

The reason you need to be familiar with the four personality types, observe others' body language, and listen to the words they frequently use is because awareness gives you a broader and more accurate picture of what motivates them to act and say what they do. There is greater awareness when you gain more knowledge and apply that knowledge to what you see and hear. While you can observe behaviors, if you don't know the cause of the behavior, it's just empty information.

You can be aware of how others stand, sit, walk, and communicate, but if you don't know what these signals mean, the information is no use to you. Your perceptions of people continue to form based on nothing more than your past experiences, which give you a limited, one-dimensional picture. When you can combine your past experiences and motivations to a greater knowledge of what's behind these behaviors and words, then your relationships will magically improve, and your actions and beliefs will change as well.

If you want to increase your awareness and apply it to your analysis of others, you've come to the right place. Educating yourself on reading body language and recognizing personality types will enable you to achieve more efficient communications with people much different from yourself. Most people tend to form relationships with individuals who are like them, so learning to monitor and adjust your behaviors and words to match another will draw others to you.

Principle #4: Position Alters Perception

All of us would like to believe that our perceptions and analysis are not unduly influenced by another's position, but the truth of the matter is that we are all impressed or turned off by others based on many different criteria. Much of what impacts our analysis has nothing to do with how they behave or what they say. Many perceptions are the results of the other person's position in life. Being influenced by another's position in life doesn't mean that every person who has a big title is automatically respected because some people resent others' success. The following are some things that alter perceptions.

- Career Choice

- Company

- Job Title

- Your Bosses' Favored-Peer

- Other Friends or Acquaintances Who Page Homage to Their Authority

If your perception of another is that they are above or below your status, then your analysis of that person will be impacted by your perception. If you review the personality types, you'll notice that Leader and Perceiver Personalities can be more judging than Fraternizers and Identifiers. Knowing you are a Leader Personality Type can help you to understand that you often allow others' positions to get in the way of your analysis and influence your beliefs about them. Gaining this knowledge about your personality type makes you more aware of how you respond to others' behaviors and beliefs, thereby creating better relationships.

Principle #5: We See What We Want to See

Have you ever noticed how what you expect to happen almost always happens? Well, this is no coincidence. Expectations influence our analysis of others' behaviors and words. In other words, we see what we want to see, especially if our emotions are involved. If we are in a highly emotional state, it's difficult to see past the anger, love, or fear.

Analysis based on emotion is not just slightly inaccurate, but those perceptions are often so slanted that when you share your thoughts with others, they think you've lost touch with reality. I'm sure you have heard of all the romance scams happening online these days. Men and women are being swindled out of hundreds of thousands of dollars because they are in a vulnerable state and allow another person to take advantage of them. There are now scammers who have developed "so-called" services that say they can help reveal a possible scammer. That's the web emotions can weave when it comes to analyzing the behaviors and motives of those we think we know.

Some people with a terminal illness believe they can be cured by a concoction provided through someone who claims to be a doctor. Unfortunately, this is what happened to Carl. Carl's specialist diagnosed him with third-stage cancer. His prognosis wasn't promising, but when Carl could not accept the hopelessness of his situation, he contacted a doctor he heard of who had experienced incredible results with his treatment of cancer. Carl spent thousands of dollars traveling to India, and thousands more staying at the doctor's treatment center. The treatments were uncomfortable, and they kept Carl away from his family for weeks at a time, but at the end of each treatment, Carl felt better for a while.

The doctor told Carl that it would take several treatments before he would experience lasting results, and each time Carl would see what he wanted to see. Although his family saw him getting weaker, thinner, and less energetic, Carl saw himself as more fit and in a calmer state of mind. Just days after his last treatment, Carl died of cancer, and his family felt cheated out of the time they could have spent with him during his final year of life. How could an otherwise intelligent, professional man have been so fooled? It's easy; he allowed his highly emotional state to override his better judgment. He wanted the treatments to work so badly, that he was victim to the fifth principle of perceptions—we see what we want to see.

The Importance of Knowing the Five Principles of Perception

To read and analyze others accurately, you must first understand how perceptions influence behaviors and beliefs and then judge the accuracy of your feelings. It just doesn't help to read one's body language if you don't realize your interpretation of your observations is skewed. All the while you are questioning others' motives, you also need to be examining yours.

Combining personality types, body language, the spoken word, and the way you form perceptions of yourself and others will give you the bigger picture—a more well-rounded view of our intentional and unintentional communications. Knowing what you know now, you can analyze others with confidence and assurance that the things observed and heard are indicative of the meanings you have attributed to them.

As you learn about how to read one's body language and listen for the verbal clues that identify one's true motives, you can attach your perceptions of the person or situation without the concerns that you have misjudged or misread their meaning. Now it's time to look at the incredible signals and signs we send out every day without being conscious of how they help others to form their perceptions of us.

CHAPTER 3

BODY LANGUAGE SPEAKS VOLUMES

Some people are naturals at reading others, but they couldn't tell you how they know what they know. That's because they are intuitively reading others' body language, but they don't have the knowledge to define why they are such good communicators. More than 70 percent of the messages we send and receive are through non-verbal language. Not only are the greatest percent of our messages non-verbal, but that non-verbal language is more honest and genuine than the words we speak. Our bodies don't sugar coat the message; we just respond and react without being conscious of doing so.

If people are saying one thing but their body language is delivering a different message, put more stock in what you see than what you hear. However, to make sure you are reading the person correctly, let's discuss all the different nonverbal messages we send. We'll cover the nonverbal signals and what they might mean, but keep in mind that different cultures and countries might attach a different meaning to your body language. When you're confused about the nonverbal message that another is sending, then listen to the words and take the signals in context with the phrases they use.

Another way to determine the message is through the tone, pitch, and volume of another's voice. It gives truth to that saying, "It's not what you said but how you said it." When all these things are examined during your analysis of others, you'll find clarity in the message. While we're at it, there is one more thing—pay attention to the other person's required personal space. If you are questioning whether the message they are sending is positive, negative, or benevolent, step inside their personal space and be aware of their reaction. Their feelings will then be quite pronounced. If the message was meant to be off-putting, they will immediately step back or adopt a space-claiming stance that will let you know their feelings in no uncertain terms.

Facial Expressions, Features, and Head Movement

- Playing with Hair and Moving the Head

If someone slides their fingers through their hair at the temples and tosses their head back, this is an indication they might be flirting with you. On the other hand, if they are running their fingers through their hair from their forehead through the top of their crown, that is a sign they are confused or frustrated. Tilting the head and twirling the hair is also a flirtatious mannerism, indicating interest combined with a little nervous tension.

When people nod their heads, it matters how many times they do so before stopping. For example, public speakers who are attentive to their audiences know that three nods mean interest and attentiveness. However, if you observe a group of people conversing, you'll notice the person who nods their head only once is eager to leave and will probably be the next one to make a quick exit.

If someone is interested in what you're saying, they will often tilt their head in your direction. They could be showing curiosity or questioning what you are saying when they bring one ear closer to make sure they are getting every detail of the conversation.

- Eye Movement

People usually blink six or seven times a minute, but those who are stressed blink quite a bit more. If someone covers their eyes with their hands, excessively rubs their eyes, or closes their eyes, they could be hiding something or feel threatened.

When the eyes are shifty or rapidly moving from one person to another, it reflects some scattered thoughts that are going on in their heads. If there is a flickering interest between two people when this is happening, then it can also be a way for people to prevent detection as they were checking out the other.

If someone has a habit of not making eye contact or looking down as they speak, it can show shyness or can also be a cry for empathy. They are waiting for you to ask what's wrong and open the way for them to share their feelings. Investigators have come to realize that a sustained glance from a person who denies involvement in a crime, may mean they are lying and trying to over-compensate by looking them straight in the eyes for a long time to show they're telling the truth.

If you have posed a question and the person you asked looks upward, they are most likely trying to picture something they saw. On the other hand, if they look to the side toward their ear, they could be trying to recall a message they heard. If they look downward after your question, they are connecting your question with something negative and trying to find a way to avoid answering or revealing their feelings about the matter.

- Eyebrow Movement

If individuals raise their eyebrows, it usually means the person is curious about or interested in your conversation. A quick popup of one eyebrow could be a flirtation, and if the eyebrow is raised a bit longer, it often means that the other person doesn't quite buy into what you say.

If the brows furrow, you can almost bet that person is having second thoughts about what is being done or said. It most likely indicates a negative emotion like fear or confusion, so it might be time for you to back off a bit.

- Lips

Of course, a smile sends a universal message, if it is truly a smile. We've all been at the other end of a fake smile, which is one that doesn't travel all the way to the eyes and make them wrinkle in agreement. We call those "Red Carpet" smiles. They are Hollywood smiles given by people who are trying to be friendly to their fans but just want to get inside, sit down, and make it through the night.

Individuals who plaster a smile on their face almost all the time, are usually nervous. If it's in the workplace, they could feel out-of-their-depth or incompetent. There's a good chance that foreigners who smile a lot don't understand a blasted thing, so they just smile and nod.

Another thing people do with their lips is to suck on them and bite them. Sucking or biting the lip is a reaction by those who need to settle themselves down. Like a newborn, the action soothes them and offers a bit of comfort in a stressful situation. If one clamps down on their lips or purses them, it can mean frustration or anger.

Body and Limb Movements

- Body Positions

If there is a group of people standing and talking and one or more people open their bodies to you, that is an invitation to join the conversation. If they just turn their head, you might want to choose another group. You will know if you have captured the attentions of a love interest because he or she will turn slightly toward you and point their feet in your direction, to indicate they are interested in finding out what makes you tick. If you step into the group and the person beside you touches your shoulder or arm, this is a direct ploy to show you they are interested in exploring the relationship a bit further.

When you step into the group, if the person beside you leans into you, they genuinely like you. If their head retracts backward, perhaps something you said surprised or offended them. If they physically lean away from you, they've already made up their mind that they're not going to listen to or like you. If they turn their head in the opposite direction and follow it with their shoulder, you just got the cold shoulder. So, forget about it!

- Standing Positions

If someone is standing with legs about shoulder width apart, it often is a sign of dominance and determination, as if they needed to stand their ground against something or prove a point. If they stand with legs together, front forward, they will hear you out, but you need to make your point quickly. When the person you are speaking with is standing and shifting their weight from side-to-side or front-to-back, it might indicate several things. They could be bored, or they are anxious and need to sooth themselves with this rocking sort of movement. To determine their feelings, it is necessary to look further at what they are doing with their arms as well.

- Arm Positions

Don't assume that crossed arms always mean that the other person is upset. Not so! Some people will stand or sit with their arms crossed because it is just a comfortable position. You can distinguish the other's emotions by looking further at their facial expression. If they have furrowed eyebrows, their mouth pursed, and their arms crossed, chances are they are angry or upset about something. Crossed arms can also be a sign of protection or a closed attitude to the ideas you are presenting.

If someone is talking with their arms flopping around, it can mean they are excited and agreeable, or it can say that they are out of control. Again, you'll need to couple your observations with other nonverbal messages to be sure. Typically, people who are overly animated are less believable and have less control over their emotions, as well as having a lack of power. They flail their arms to gain attention as if to say "I'm talking now, so would somebody please listen to me?"

- Leg and Foot Positions

People whose toes turn inward could be closing themselves off to your comments, or they could just be pigeon-toed. To determine if there is a physiological issue that causes their toes to point it, you might need more background information. Don't rush to judgment, just wait, observe more body language, and listen to their words. Some people who began turning in their toes because they were insecure or awkward, might have created a habit that they find difficult to break. The only message they are sending is one that says; I have a physical issue that is impacting my body language.

- Sitting Positions

If a person is spread out all over your couch, they have a feeling of self-importance. On the other hand, they probably have a good deal of confidence as well. Legs open, leaning forward with elbows on knees shows an in-charge attitude that is still open to hearing what you have to say.

If a person is sitting next to you and crosses their legs at the knee, pointing their foot toward you, they are giving you permission to approach them. If, however, they are sitting next to you and angle their body in the opposite direction, you're probably not going to engage or connect with him or her. If that same person is fidgeting, quickly moving their ankle or foot, they are looking for a way out. Excuse yourself; both of you will probably feel more comfortable.

- Hands

When people sit on their hands, and the temperatures aren't below freezing, it could be an indication that they are deceitful—trying to hide something from you. If they walk with their hands in their pockets or behind their back, they might be relaying information, but you're not getting the full picture because they are withholding information. When you look at one's fingers and see bitten nails or chewed cuticles, you can bet that is a nervous person with low self-esteem. Or else they have put themselves in a situation that they find extremely uncomfortable.

When someone holds their hands like a church steeple and presses them to their lips, they have something important to add to the conversation but are trying to decide how to present their information. They are self-assured and will contribute when the time is right. These are the thinkers, the analytical types.

If the person is rubbing their legs with open palms pressed down, they are feeling vulnerable or uncomfortable with your nearness or your conversation. If nothing is said, don't think you are not sending a message that is perhaps louder than any words. Examine your body language and see what message you are sending to them that could be creating this reaction.

- Walking

People who advance with rather large strides are purposeful and perceived as important and competent. People think those who walk with a little bounce in their step most likely have a positive nature. And those who walk hunched over with shoulders down—well, that kind of speaks for itself, doesn't it? They are probably prone to depression and wrapped a bit too tight.

What Does One's Voice Say About Them?

There are four indicators of the quality of one's voice. They are one's intonation, volume, pitch, and rate of speech. If the voice is monotone and rather flat, they are probably bored or boring. The lack of animation in the voice could also indicate the speaker is tired. If the person's voice sounds clear and concise, they most usually are confident and powerful, more like the Leader Personality Type. If the volume is quiet or soft, the person is thought to be shy, or it could even mean they have a secret they don't want to share.

The rate of speech is also quite important when analyzing others, especially if you are attempting to mirror them to increase the chances of connectivity. For example, Leader Personality Types will usually speak fast and loud, and you need to match their volume and rate. Identifiers often speak slower than Leaders, and their pitch is more soothing than the dominant personality type. The voice can be a strong descriptive element of the individual's personality type.

By now, you have probably caught on that every movement has a message. Verify the meaning of some of the nonverbal languages by other things, such as one's words, voice, facial expressions, and gestures. To discover one's real message, you must become a student of human behavior, studying the other's movements, speech pattern, attitude, words, gestures, and expressions to analyze people successfully.

You've been introduced to the nonverbal language and the four main personality types, and to how you form accurate perceptions, but all these things are not separate from one another. They all blend to create effective communications. In the next chapter, you'll be asked to read some scenarios and identify the personality types, nonverbal indicators, and interpret the intended message.

CHAPTER 4

INTERPRETING AND RESPONDING TO THE MESSAGE

You've already learned how to analyze nonverbal language, but the key to excellent communications is knowing how to interpret and respond to the messages others send so that you can connect with them on a much more effective level. Wouldn't it be wonderful not to wonder what a person is thinking? Instead of questioning whether people are agreeable or accepting of your suggestions or opinions, you can use all the strategies you have learned in this book to look beyond the spoken word and read the hidden feelings people might be entertaining.

Some personality types are naturally more suited to one another, while others trigger feelings of annoyance and impatience, depending upon their key traits and character preferences. By examining each personality type a bit further, you'll gain some insight into why you instantly hit it off with some people and others just rub you the wrong way.

Leaders with Other Leaders

Partnering two Leader Personality Types is like putting two alpha dogs together in the same arena. Each one fights to lead, with nobody left to follow through and complete the task. With such competitive natures, Leaders struggle with one another to manipulate and control their environment. They are both sure their strategies and methodologies are the best, and compromise is not one of their strengths. For these reasons, placing two Leaders on a project can create unnecessary power plays, unless one's secondary personality type is a Fraternizer or Identifier.

When the relationship is personal, a coupling of two Leaders can be all work and no fun. If each is career-minded individuals, your lives will most likely not revolve around each other, but be centered on work-related events and projects. It is common when two career professionals hook up, for a while they will be quite intrigued by one another's focus and business acumen. However, as the relationship matures, the Leaders will tend to be more attentive to work-related issues, and their personal relationships suffer. If you are a Leader involved with another Leader Personality Type, you'll need to challenge one another on a personal level to keep the fires burning. Compete in a mutually enjoyed sport, or find a thrill-seeking, competitive hobby that interest both of you. It's necessary to be involved in one another's home life as well as your business endeavors.

Leaders with Perceivers

Leaders usually work well with Perceiver Personality Types because they are organizers and analytical thinkers, and their quiet, unemotional demeanor typically satisfies the Leader's goal-driven manner. The Perceiver doesn't challenge the Leader for "top dog" position because he or she doesn't enjoy being the center of attention. The downside to partnering a Leader with a Perceiver is that the professional or personal relationship can be cold and rather unexciting unless there are some Fraternizer traits in one or the other's personality.

Leaders with Fraternizers or Identifiers

If the Fraternizers or Identifiers have some secondary Perceiver or Leader traits, they will do well when relating to people who are almost all Leader types. However, if the Fraternizer or Identifier is strong in their personality traits, their empathetic and emotional behaviors will often grate on the Leader's last nerve. What Fraternizers and Identifiers need to do when communicating with a Leader or Perceiver Types is to learn to curb their feelings and reign in their emotions when interacting with these strong personalities.

The two personality types that are usually not good to put together are Leader to Leader and Fraternizer to Fraternizer, and here's why. As we said before, two Leaders will fight for the controlling position. Examining the Fraternizers, they too are competitive, and they will experience a struggle unique to their type. Fraternizers will almost always try to one-up each other, challenging one another to a more dangerous sport or a project that requires greater and greater risks. Or, Fraternizers will turn everything into such fun that there will be no work accomplished. So, let's examine how to respond best to each personality type.

Communicating with an Identifier

Avoid getting too emotional when talking with an Identifier Personality Type. Since they are rather indecisive, you'll need to continually pull them back to the task at hand and discuss the decision to make and its' probably outcome. Identifiers enjoy talking about feelings, and they will be sensitive to yours. While this is good in a personal relationship, in the office it can be distracting.

If the Identifier is your direct report, their open-door policy will enable others to frequently interrupt your time with them, creating difficulties when trying to get them to stay on task. So, be patient; your frustration will not change their policies; it will only serve to make you look grumpy and cynical. After their interruptions, they'll be tempted to discuss the other person's problems with you, which will take you further down the rabbit hole. So, count on your meetings with Identifiers taking longer and achieving less.

There is almost always delays in projects as well. The Identifier will want you to check with other team members to see how they feel about any new ideas or changes, no matter how seemingly insignificant. Or, they will insist on discussing this issue in another meeting with more managers and team members. If you aren't careful, beginning a project can take a month of meetings.

In your personal relationships, Identifiers can be a bit moody and overly sensitive. If you are a Leader personality involved with a significant other who is an Identifier, you need to get comfortable with a relationship that is emotionally demanding. Also, your need to stay focused and move forward may make them feel as though they are not being heard or valued. As a Leader, you will need to slow down and allow the Identifier to fulfill his or her need to nurture and comfort. You won't be allowed to hide away when you're sick, and too many evenings spent working at the office is going to create some emotional outbursts.

Communicating with a Perceiver

Being in a personal relationship with a Perceiver Personality Type can be a guessing game. They don't like to share their feelings, and they can be a bit stand-offish, so if you are an Identifier that needs more reassurance, just know that you're not going to get it from the Perceiver. They might have deep feelings for you, but sharing those feelings is a challenge for them.

On the other hand, if you show too many emotions in the relationship, they'll be confused and draw further back into their comfortable, quiet shell of self-protection. Perceivers can also be rather stubborn and set in their ways, so getting them to change is like pulling teeth. If you do expect change, make sure you give them plenty of time to think things through and avoid popping any surprises on them, no matter how pleasant you think it will be for them to experience the change.

For example, Laurie decided it would be a great birthday present to replace her husband, Al's football chair. It was embarrassingly worn, and the springs were giving way, so she felt he would be much more comfortable watching his favorite programs in a nice, cushy, new recliner. As a surprise, Laurie had the new chair delivered while Al was at work, and they took the tattered one away. She didn't quite get the reaction she was hoping for when Al returned from work. Although he has never complained much about his old chair, Al has merely changed his favorite seating area to a corner of the couch.

Al might have liked the idea of having a new chair had Laurie not surprised him with the idea and had his old one hauled away before he was ready for the change. He needed time to adjust to the idea that another chair could be just as comfortable, and he could have gone to the store, sat in a gazillion chairs, then slowly made his mind up to purchase the first one in which he plopped. However, without having the opportunity to think it over, look at the chairs to decide which one best suited him, and then compare prices and warranties, Al was not thrilled with Laurie's birthday present

Communicating with a Fraternizer

Fraternizer Personality Types can get along with almost anyone, but some personality types will eventually grow weary of their tired jokes and constant need for entertainment. Also, a Perceiver will not appreciate the spontaneous spending that many Fraternizers practice. A died-in-the-wool Fraternizer with few secondary personality traits that are more grounded is often too immature and impulsive for a Leader of Perceiver in their personal relationships.

In the workplace, Fraternizers are often perceived as party people and not taken seriously. No matter how intelligent, many Fraternizers are not promoted to their potential because they allow their fun-loving spirit too much free reign in the workplace. Fraternizers usually don't make good quarterly budget planners because they spend too freely and are too rash when it comes to decision-making. If you work with a Fraternizer, you will need to keep them focused and grounded to achieve success with projects in which you are both involved.

Examining Some Personal Scenarios

Think of a co-working with whom you are currently experiencing some challenges when communicating with him or her. Now review the following questions to determine the other person's personality type and what you can do to create a more positive working relationship.

- What is your subject's dominant personality type? How do you know this?

- What is your dominant personality type?

- What does this person do that annoys you? Analyze these behaviors to see if this is a trait of their personality type?

- What do you think you are doing that annoys him or her?

- Is this your imagination, or are you reading their non-verbal language?

- What was the last challenge you experienced with him or her?

- Based on his or her personality type, how could you have responded better to create a more positive outcome?

- Knowing what you know now, how will you communicate with this person in the future to create a better relationship?

Now, think of a personal relationship you would like to improve and ask yourself the same questions. When you determine the other's personality type, make sure you verify your beliefs by observing their behaviors, listening to their words, and analyzing the body language they are displaying around you. Ask yourself if you are too sensitive because of your personality type, or if you really are having serious communication issues with this person.

If you cannot answer the questions about people who challenge you, then keep reading. The next chapter will deal with Three Key Elements to Connectivity, which will give you some useful tools to help you to analyze others accurately.

CHAPTER 5

Three Key Elements to Connectivity

There are three critical key elements to one's ability to successfully connect with others: mindful observation, listening with intent, and effective feedback.

Connecting with Others Through Mindful Observation

So, what is meant by mindful observation? Like most of us, you observe people and your surroundings all the time, but what do you take away from the things you see? How do you apply what you see to help you monitor and adjust your behaviors and beliefs? The reality is, most people use very little of what they see to improve their communications. If they are more aware than most, they might see that what they are saying is not being well received by their audience. Consequently, they just stop communicating. Most people make very few adjustments to improve their communications. Instead, they only pass the baton to the next person in the conversation who is eager to participate.

In most instances, there is no monitoring and adjusting of verbal and non-verbal language because many individuals have never learned how to analyze people and adjust their communication style to be more accommodating to that person's personality type. The powers of observation can only help when people put what they see to work and create a more active exchange of information.

To improve your observation skills, you need to work like a dog! You heard—just like a dog. Dogs have amazing observation skills. In fact, trainers say that the best way to teach a dog to do the trick is by letting them see another dog perform it and receive a reward. A dog's observation skills are so keen that they learn better by watching than by verbal commands. Who's to say the same thing isn't so for humans?

Marsha's dog is so observant, Hannah knows what she'll be doing that day based on the things she observes her owner doing. For example, if Marsha pulls out her running shoes, Hannah knows they are going for a run. If Marsha pulls her hair back into a ponytail, Hannah suspects they are going herding and runs into the garage to wait at the car door because Marsha always wears her hair in a ponytail when she takes Hannah herding.

The problem comes when Marsha decides to pull her hair into a ponytail, and she's not taking Hannah herding. Hannah is so sure she's going herding that she begins to scratch and pester Marsha as if to ask why she pulled the switch. Hannah is relentless in her attempts to get Marsha to do as she wants, confident they'll be leaving soon. Hannah's so sure of her ability to read her owner that she will stand at the garage door for almost an hour waiting for Marsha's approach. The problem is, although Hannah read all the signs, she didn't know that the same sign could have several meanings.

The reason I tell this story is to warn you that sometimes you can have excellent observation skills and yet with this one person this one time, they don't work. What you observe and attach meaning to isn't want was intended. You keep doing the same thing, and yet you aren't getting the results you want. Your communication isn't improving, and neither is your relationship. When this happens, change things. Don't assume the same thing works for all people. Try something different to get to better communications. The most important aspect to remember is that giving up gets you nowhere.

Sometimes you just need to observe a little longer or a bit more. Don't' just see the person as they communicate with you, watch how they communicate with others. Watch how others react to them. If this is a person with whom you have issues, watch their body language around those you know they like. Listen to their voice as they speak with others with whom they communicate well. Then observe how that other person responds to the one with whom you have issues. How does their voice sound? What is their body language saying? How are they standing or sitting that is different from the way you respond? For complicated relationships, surface observations just aren't enough.

You must be mindful of your goal as you observe your subject. What is it you want from the relationship? Being aware means you can't always focus on all things going on around them, but you need to choose just one or two things to observe for a while until you have a greater understanding of what they are saying with that gesture or expression. Once you know that, then move on to something else. Being mindful in your observations means you are determined to resolve the situation and improve the communications with that person.

Listening with Intent

Just as people observe others every day, they also hear them as well. The downside is you can hear someone, but if you are listening with a specific intent, you won't know what to do with what you hear. For instance, you can hear someone speaking, but if you are not listening with the intent to distinguish the person's rate of speech when they are talking or the volume of which they speak with a plan to identify their personality type, then you hear only part of the message.

When listening with intent, you don't interrupt, you don't plan what you're going to say next while the other is still talking, and you don't speak over that person. In fact, you don't speak at all; you listen, and you listen with the intent of discovering the meaning behind the words and between the lines.

Giving Effective Feedback

Sometimes providing effective feedback is nothing more than mimicking a person's rate or volume of speech. At other times, useful feedback means adopting an open, relaxed stance to reflect what you would like to see the other person do as well. Then there are times effective feedback means adjusting your personality traits a bit so that you don't make the other person uncomfortable or annoyed. If your message is garbled because your body language, gestures, and expressions are different from your words, then you need to bring clarity to the conversation by providing congruent feedback.

Of course, there are times where you don't want people to read what you are thinking, and in that case, effective feedback will be that which masks the way you feel. It is not about hiding your feelings, but more liked controlling them. It's not beneficial to you or anyone else if you always reveal every single thought and feeling. There are times you need to bury your emotions a bit so that your communications don't expose you or put you in a vulnerable position. In these cases, effective feedback is NOT revealing what you don't want another to know.

Practice these three key elements to connectivity and others will not only feel connected to you, but they will be more supportive of your ideas and suggestions. It's a way to get what you want without emotional outbursts and unreasonable demands. You get your way because you are an outstanding communicator. You get the support of others because they like you and because you GET them. You achieve success in your personal and professional life because you connect with others and they with you, and all because of the few strategies you've learned from these pages. Don't look now, but you've just practiced the three key elements to connectivity: mindful observation, listening with intent, and providing effective feedback.

CHAPTER 6

THE BEAUTY OF SUCCESSFULLY ANALYZING OTHERS

What a thrill it is to learn to analyze others and stop the anxiety of wondering how someone feels about you or what they think of your ideas or suggestions. Learning how to read someone's body language is as exciting as learning how to understand the author's meaning in a book or interpret a foreign language. What will help you to continue practicing and improving your analytical skills is to understand that you don't become an expert at reading others overnight. It takes time, practice, and a willingness to adopt good listening and observation skills to become an exceptional communicator.

There are tremendous payoffs that come from successfully analyzing others. The better you get, the more friends you'll have because people gravitate to those they like. The more you practice the strategies learned in this book, the better you'll get at reading people and adjusting your behaviors and language to match others. Soon analyzing one's body language and gestures will become second nature to you, and you'll wonder why you failed to notice the distinctive messages the body sends long before now.

Many aspects of your life will improve along with your communications. You'll have opportunities offered, and doors opened that were previously always out of reach. You'll see the world differently because the world will see you differently as well. Your confidence and self-esteem will raise with your increased ability to accurately analyze others. People will gain a new appreciation of you, and you'll be asked to participate in work projects or on teams whose members before may not have chosen you as a player.

There's magic in excellent communications, and that magic is making meaningful, long-lasting relationships. You'll look back on those people who you once considered the "beautiful" people and suddenly realize that you have joined their ranks. It may sound far-fetched, but our entire lives revolve around our ability to connect with others by speaking their language, by understanding the message they are sending, and by offering feedback that supports and enhances others.

One of the best feelings you can create in another person is that they are better off for having known you, for having kept company with you, and that's what learning to analyze people can do. People will leave your presence feeling good about spending time with you. You will leave the company of others without concern that your message wasn't understood or appreciated. Analyzing others is a work of art—a work of beauty—a treasure of information to be studied, enjoyed and shared.

CONCLUSION

CONGRATULATIONS ON YOUR READ

Thank you so much for purchasing this book!

I hope reading *How to Analyze People: How to Master Reading Anyone Instantly Using Body Language, Human Psychology, and Personality Types* will help you to improve your personal and professional communications significantly.

The next step is to put these strategies to work in your life to create great relationships.

Once again, don't forget to grab a copy of your FREE BONUS book *"The Secrets Behind Subtle Psychology: Secrets To Getting All You Want"*. If you are interested in learning more about human psychology and being more effective in conversations, then this book is for you.

Just go to http://bit.ly/subtlepsychology

Lastly, if you enjoyed reading the book, could you please take time to share your views with us by posting a review? Having a positive review from you helps the book reach many more people, so we can continue to reach those who can benefit from the information shared within the book. It'd be highly appreciated!

Thank you and good luck on your new skills of analyzing people.

www.ingramcontent.com/pod-product-compliance
Lightning Source LLC
Chambersburg PA
CBHW071722020426
42333CB00017B/2365